SYMMETRY

Lynn Peppas

Crabtree Publishing Company
www.crabtreebooks.com

Author: Lynn Peppas
Coordinating editor: Chester Fisher
Series editor: Penny Dowdy
Editor: Reagan Miller
Proofreader: Ellen Rodger
Editorial director: Kathy Middleton
Production coordinator: Margaret Amy Salter
Prepress technician: Margaret Amy Salter
Cover design: Samara Parent
Logo design: Samantha Crabtree
Project manager: Kumar Kunal (Q2AMEDIA)
Art direction: Dibakar Acharjee (Q2AMEDIA)
Design: Harleen Mehta (Q2AMEDIA)
Photo research: Anju Pathak (Q2AMEDIA)

Photographs:
BigStockPhoto: Elena Elisseeva: p. 5; Alexey Popov: p. 17 (right)
Istockphoto: p. 11; Roger Bucher: p. 15; Donald Erickson:
    p. 17 (bottom left); Jill Lang: p. 1; Robyn Mackenzie: p. 6;
    Peter Spiro: p. 19; Ron Summers: p. 4; Sami Suni: p. 21;
    Lisa Thornberg: p. 19
Q2AMedia Art Bank: p. 5, 7, 8, 9, 11, 12, 13, 15, 19, 20, 21, 23
Shutterstock: p. 10, 13, 18 (top), 23; Sipos András: p. 15;
    Galina Barskaya: p. 17 (top left); Yuri Bershadsky: p. 19;
    Neo Edmund: front cover (bottom right); Fotosav:
    p. 18 (bottom); Mates: p. 9; Andrew Park: p. 15; Cora
    Reed: p. 7; Kimberly Ann Reinick: p. 14 (right); Juan
    Jose Rodriguez Velandia: p. 13; Carlos E. Santa Maria:
    p. 14 (left); Lori Sparkia: front cover (center); Szefei: p. 19

Library and Archives Canada Cataloguing in Publication

Peppas, Lynn
      Symmetry / Lynn Peppas.

(My path to math)
Includes index.
ISBN 978-0-7787-4351-4 (bound).--ISBN 978-0-7787-4369-9 (pbk.)

      1. Symmetry (Mathematics)--Juvenile literature. I. Title.
II. Series: My path to math

QA174.7.S96P46 2009   j516'.1   C2009-903582-0

Library of Congress Cataloging-in-Publication Data

Peppas, Lynn.
    Symmetry / Lynn Peppas.
        p. cm. -- (My path to math)
    Includes index.
    ISBN 978-0-7787-4351-4 (reinforced lib. bdg. : alk. paper)
    -- ISBN 978-0-7787-4369-9 (pbk. : alk. paper)
      1. Symmetry (Mathematics)--Juvenile literature. I. Title.

    QA174.7.S96.P46 2010
    516'.1--dc22
                                              2009022858

Crabtree Publishing Company

www.crabtreebooks.com   1-800-387-7650

Published in Canada
Crabtree Publishing
616 Welland Ave.
St. Catharines, ON
L2M 5V6

Published in the United States
Crabtree Publishing
PMB16A
350 Fifth Ave., Suite 3308
New York, NY 10118

Published in the United Kingdom
Crabtree Publishing
Lorna House, Suite 3.03, Lorna Road
Hove, East Sussex, UK
BN3 3EL

Published in Australia
Crabtree Publishing
386 Mt. Alexander Rd.
Ascot Vale (Melbourne)
VIC 3032

Contents

Symmetry

Nick helps his dad fold clothes. He folds a blue shirt. He folds it down the middle. He flips one side so it fits against the other. Now both sides look the same. It looks like half of a shirt. The shirt has **line symmetry**.

Something has line symmetry when it can be folded and both sides match up.

folding line

Activity Box

Place a small pocket mirror along the dotted line on the picture of Nick's folded shirt. What do you see? A mirror image shows symmetry.

We can find things that have symmetry when we fold clothes.

Lines of Symmetry

A **line of symmetry** is a folding line that makes both sides of something meet up.

Nick folds a washcloth. He uses a **vertical** fold line. Both sides **match**. He uses a **horizontal** fold line. Both sides match. He uses a **diagonal** fold line. Both sides are the same again. The washcloth has four lines of symmetry.

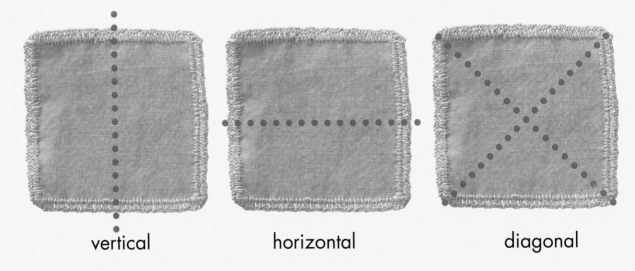

vertical   horizontal   diagonal

Fact Box

Objects can have more than one line of symmetry.

Nick's washcloth can be folded four
different ways to show symmetry.

No Symmetry

Sometimes things do not have symmetry. Nick folds his shirt with a horizontal line. But the sides do not line up. This is not a line of symmetry. He makes a diagonal fold. But the sides do not match. Nick's shirt has one line of symmetry. It is the vertical folding line.

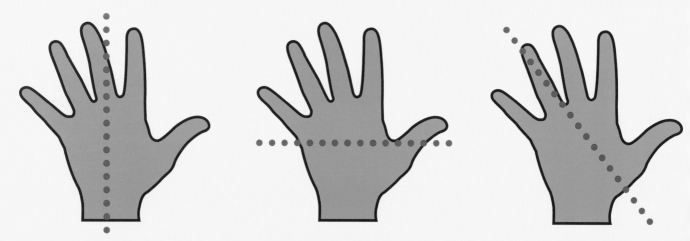

Activity Box

Trace your hand on a piece of paper. Cut the shape out. Try a vertical, horizontal, or diagonal line of symmetry. Does your hand have symmetry?

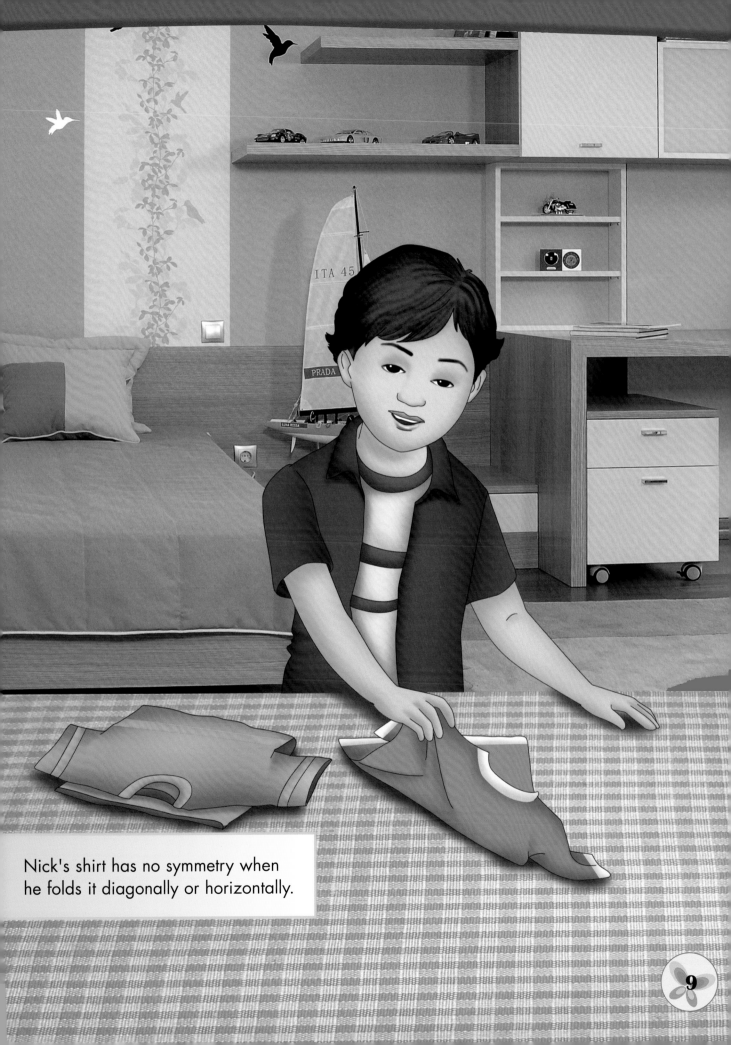

Nick's shirt has no symmetry when he folds it diagonally or horizontally.

Turns

Things that turn can have symmetry too. The fan on the opposite page has three arms called blades. The fan blades turn slowly. The blades look the same three times as it makes one full turn. The fan has **point symmetry**. When an object has point symmetry, it looks the same when it turns less than an entire circle. What happens when we turn the hands of the clock? The hands look the same only one time. It does not have point symmetry.

▶ The clock does not have point symmetry. The hands will not look this way again until they both go all the way around.

Fact Box

If a shape matches only one time after a full turn, it does not have point symmetry.

During one turn, the three blades on this fan match three times.

Alphabet Symmetry

Nick sees that many things can have symmetry. Even letters can have symmetry. He writes a B on the chalkboard. Nick imagines a horizontal line of symmetry runs through it. The letter B has symmetry. Not all letters have symmetry. Nick tries to find lines of symmetry for P. But it has no symmetry.

Activity Box

Look at the letters D, H, G, T, A. Which letters have line symmetry? What letter has point symmetry too?

Draw some letters on a chalkboard or a piece of paper. Do they have symmetry?

13

Symmetry of Shapes

Nick looks through the school bus window. He sees that street signs can have symmetry. A stop sign is in a shape called an **octagon**. It has eight **equal** sides with eight equal **angles**. A stop sign has eight lines of symmetry. Now turn the stop sign one full turn. The stop sign lines up eight times. It has point symmetry, too.

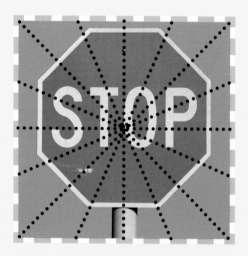

Activity Box

What shape is the yield sign? How many lines of symmetry does it have? How many times does the triangle line up in one full turn?

14

This street sign has point and line symmetry!

Buildings Symmetry

Buildings can have symmetry too. Imagine a vertical line of symmetry between the middle of this house. Imagine folding both sides together along the fold line. The two sides would match. This house has symmetry. Look at the giant skyscraper. Imagine folding it along a vertical line of symmetry. Both sides would be the same. The skyscraper has symmetry.

Activity Box

This church has symmetry too. Does it have a vertical, horizontal, or diagonal line of symmetry?

Some churches, homes, and even skyscrapers can have symmetry!

Nature Symmetry

Nick visits the butterfly center. Inside he sees plants and butterflies. In nature, many living things have symmetry. When this butterfly closes its wings both sides match. It has line symmetry. The flowers have symmetry too. When we turn this flower one full time, there are many points where it matches. It has point symmetry.

Activity Box

What other things in the picture have symmetry?

Many things in nature have symmetry.
Look for things with symmetry during
your next nature walk.

Now You Try!

Nick makes a design with pattern blocks. He makes his design on one side of a vertical line. Then he makes the same design on the other side of the line. Nick's pattern has line symmetry! Does it have point symmetry? When he turns the pattern in one full circle, the points match three times. Nick's pattern has point symmetry too.

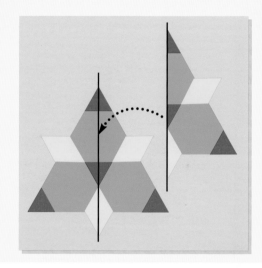

Activity Box

Draw a vertical line on a piece of paper. Place pattern blocks on one side of the line. Now place the exact same blocks in the same position but on the other side of the line. Remember to turn your pattern. Your design has symmetry!

You can make your own
pattern to show symmetry!

Glossary

angle The space or corner where two lines meet

diagonal A straight line that joins one corner of something to the other corner

equal Two or more amounts that are the same

horizontal A straight line that runs from side to side

line of symmetry A folding line that makes both sides of something meet up

line symmetry Something that can be folded and both sides match

match Something that looks the same when put together

octagon A closed shape with eight sides and eight angles

point symmetry When lines and angles match at least twice as a shape is turned once

vertical A straight line that runs through the middle of something from top to bottom

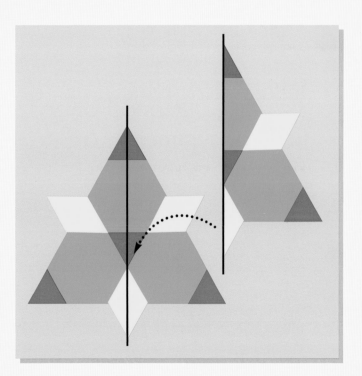

Index

Printed in the U.S.A. — BG